A Year at the Fairgrounds:
Finding Volume

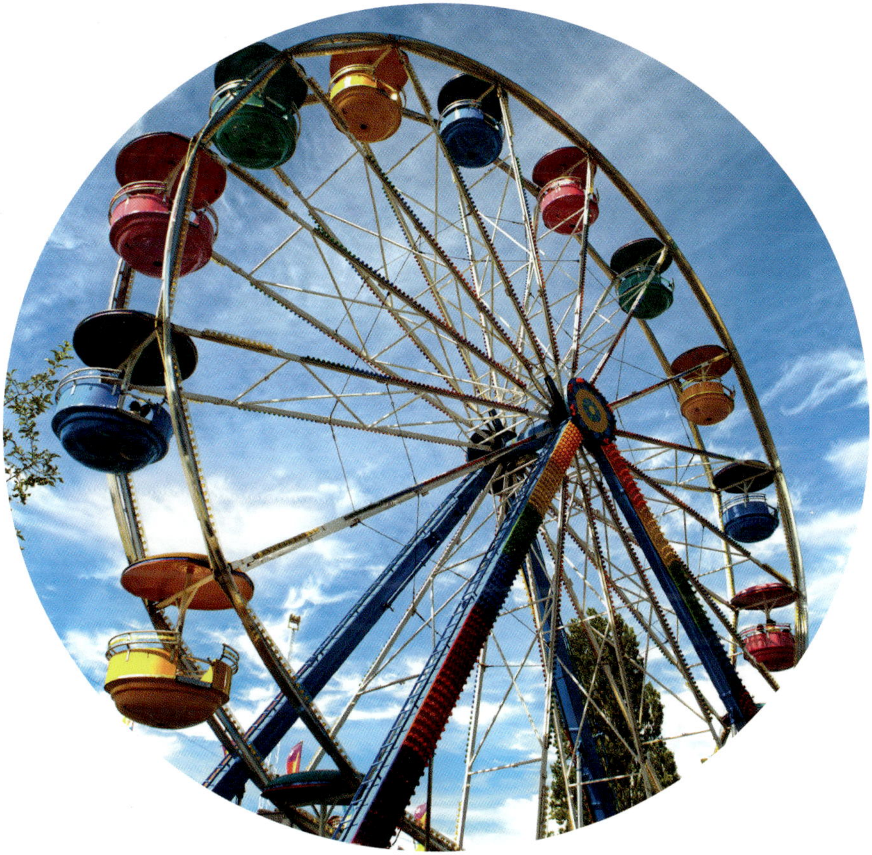

by Renata Brunner-Jass

Content Consultant
David T. Hughes
Mathematics Curriculum Specialist

Chicago, IL

Norwood House Press
PO Box 316598
Chicago, IL 60631

For information regarding Norwood House Press, please visit our website at www.norwoodhousepress.com or call 866-565-2900.

Special thanks to: Heidi Doyle
Production Management: Six Red Marbles
Editors: Linda Bullock and Kendra Muntz
Manufactured in the United States of America in North Mankato, Minnesota.
296R—082016

This book was manufactured as a paperback edition. If you are purchasing this book as a rebound hardcover or without any cover, the publisher and any licensors' rights are being violated.

Paperback ISBN: 978-1-60357-514-0

The Library of Congress has cataloged the original hardcover edition with the following call number: 2012035769

© 2013 by Norwood House Press. All Rights Reserved.

No part of this book may be reproduced without written permission from the publisher.

CONTENTS

iMath Ideas: How Much Space?	6
Discover Activity: How Many? How Much?	10
In the Fall	12
Deliveries	18
Winter Wonders	20
Math at Work	23
Spring Blooms	24
Connecting to History	30
Here Comes Summer	32
The Main Event	36
iMath Ideas: What's the Volume?	42
What Comes Next?	45
Glossary	46
Further Reading/Additional Notes	47
Index	48

Note to Caregivers:

Throughout this book, many questions are posed to the reader. Some are open-ended and ask what the reader thinks. Discuss these questions with your child and guide him or her in thinking through the possible answers and outcomes. There are also questions posed which have a specific answer. Encourage your child to read through the text to determine the correct answer. Most importantly, encourage answers grounded in reality while also allowing imaginations to soar. Information to help support you as you share the book with your child is provided in the back in the **Additional Notes** section.

Bold words are defined in the glossary in the back of the book.

A Fair Contest

Each year, millions of people attend state fairs. Many come to compete. Some enter **livestock** like sheep and goats into best-of-show contests. Others enter homemade jams and jellies, baked foods, and honey. Still others enter contests for handmade craft items, such as quilts. Everyone who enters hopes to win a ribbon that says "Best in the State."

State fairs have grown and changed over time. Many now have carnival rides and games. Ferris wheels are popular rides at many fairs. Fairs often have pony rides for younger children. Anyone can try to win toys and other prizes at carnival games. And of course, a fair wouldn't be a fair without good things to eat!

But the state fair only lasts for a few weeks or a month. What happens at a fairground during the rest of the year? Fairgrounds can, in fact, be busy places all year round.

iMath IDEAS:

How Much Space?

Some fairgrounds host monthly events. Each event requires careful planning.

Whether they are planning a small exhibit of farm animals or a concert that may attract hundreds of fans, event planners have to know a lot about space. That's because they decide where to put events within the fairgrounds.

In addition to space, events need supplies and materials, too. Knowing how much space these things require is something event planners figure out.

When planners think about how much space an object takes up, or how many **cubic units** will fill it, they are thinking about **volume**. A cubic unit is a cube with sides of equal length. There are different ways to find volume.

An event planner works with many people and collects a lot of information to plan a successful event.

Idea 1: We can **model** volume. A box has three **dimensions**, meaning it has length, width, and height. We can fill a box with cubes to determine its volume.

For example, a box holds the exact number of cubes you see below. Each cube has a volume of one cubic inch. That means it takes up one cubic inch of space.

The box holds 27 cubes in all. So, its volume is 27 cubic inches, or 27 in^3. It takes up 27 cubic inches (in^3) of space.

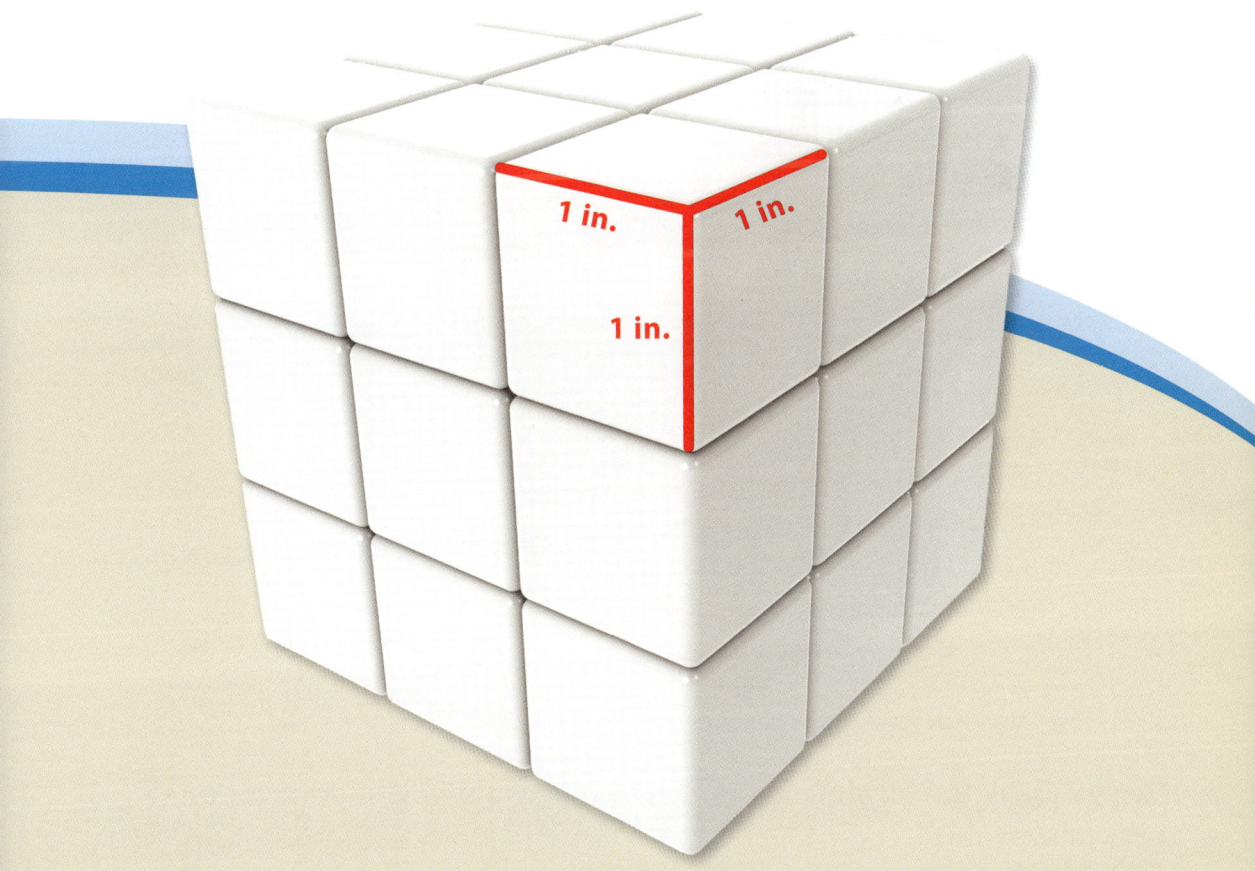

Idea 2: We can use a **formula** to find the volume of an object. A formula is a mathematical rule written with symbols.

Many boxes are examples of **rectangular prisms**. A rectangular prism has six rectangular **faces**, or sides.

The volume (V) of a rectangular prism is equal to its length (l) times its width (w) times its height (h). The formula is: $V = \ell \times w \times h$

For example, a box measures 16 inches long, 10 inches wide, and 10 inches tall. What is its volume?

$V = \ell \times w \times h$

$V = 16$ inches $\times$ 10 inches $\times$ 10 inches $= 1{,}600$ cubic inches (in^3)

The box takes up 1,600 cubic inches (in^3) of space.

Do you think the formula $V = \ell \times w \times h$ is useful for finding volume? Why or why not?

Idea 3: Use **operations.** Sometimes, we need to use an **operation** like addition, subtraction, multiplication, or division to find volume.

For example, say we want to know the volume of the object in the photograph. The object contains 10 wooden cubes. Each side of each cube is two inches long. We can use a formula to find the volume of one wooden cube.

$$2 \text{ inches} \times 2 \text{ inches} \times 2 \text{ inches} = 8 \text{ cubic inches (in}^3)$$

Then, we can use an operation to find the volume of the object.

1) We can add to find the answer:

$$8 \text{ (in}^3) + 8 \text{ (in}^3) + 8 \text{ (in}^3) + 8 \text{ (in}^3) + 8 \text{ (in}^3) + 8 \text{ (in}^3) + 8 \text{ (in}^3) + 8 \text{ (in}^3) + 8 \text{ (in}^3) + 8 \text{ (in}^3) = 80 \text{ cubic inches (in}^3)$$

2) We can multiply to find the answer.

$$8 \text{ in}^3 \times 10 \text{ cubes} = 80 \text{ cubic inches (in}^3).$$

The object takes up 80 cubic inches (in³) of space.

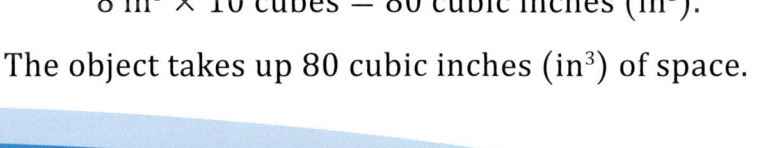

Do you think finding and using operations to find the volume of a solid figure is useful? Why or why not?

Do you think modeling is a good way to find volume? Why or why not?

DISCOVER ACTIVITY

How Many? How Much?

Materials
- several cardboard boxes, such as cereal boxes
- scissors
- ruler
- paper
- pencil

Cut one side off a cardboard box. This gives you an open-ended rectangular prism. You are looking directly into the prism.

Fit blocks or cubes neatly inside the prism, filling in most, but not all, of the space. Count the cubes that fill the box. Then, **estimate**, or make a reasonable guess, how many more cubes would fill the box completely.

Record the volume of your prism in terms of cubic units. Then, measure one of the cubes. Calculate the volume of the prism again. But this time, use the actual measurements of the cubes you used.

Next, use another method to find the volume of the prism. Will you:

- use the formula $V = \ell \times w \times h$?
- use an operation?

Use a different box to repeat the activity. Compare volumes.

In the Fall

The calendar for a fairground often includes a horse show in the fall season. Horses and their riders may compete in several different events at a horse show.

One event is **dressage**. The French word means "training." Dressage requires many hours of training and hard athletic work from both the horse and the rider. In dressage, a rider and her horse complete a series of movements. Movements may include galloping and stepping sideways. Some people call dressage "horse ballet."

Other events include jumping and cross-country racing. There is also a sport called horse ball, which is a bit like basketball. Players handle a ball and shoot it into a net—while riding horses.

Among other things, how much a horse eats and drinks depends on its size and how active it is. Horses are usually let out into a field to graze on grass as much as possible. People may give their horses additional food each day, like hay, oats, and a mixture of grains and other foods. This mixture is called "feed."

Hay is probably the best known of horse foods. Hay is sold in bundles called "bales." The size of one bale depends on the machine used to pack it.

A horse owner stacks four hay bales of equal size. Each bale is 36 inches long, 24 inches wide, and 18 inches tall. What is the volume of one bale? What is the volume of the stack of hay bales?

Another fall activity is the thrilling corn **maze**. A maze is a kind of puzzle. It has an entrance and an exit. Inside are several connected paths. But not all paths connect to others. People enter a maze and then find their way through it to the exit.

To make a corn maze, fairground workers plant a field of corn in late May. When the corn is grown, the cobs are harvested. The stalks are left to dry. Then, workers cut paths to make the maze.

The stalks that are cut to make paths are stored in a shed to use elsewhere in the park. A shed measures 12 feet by 10 feet. The height from the shed's floor to where the roof begins is 10 feet. How many cubic feet of corn stalks can the shed hold?

After cutting several paths, fairground workers store 800 cubic feet (ft^3) of corn stalks in the shed. How many more cubic feet of corn stalks can the shed hold?

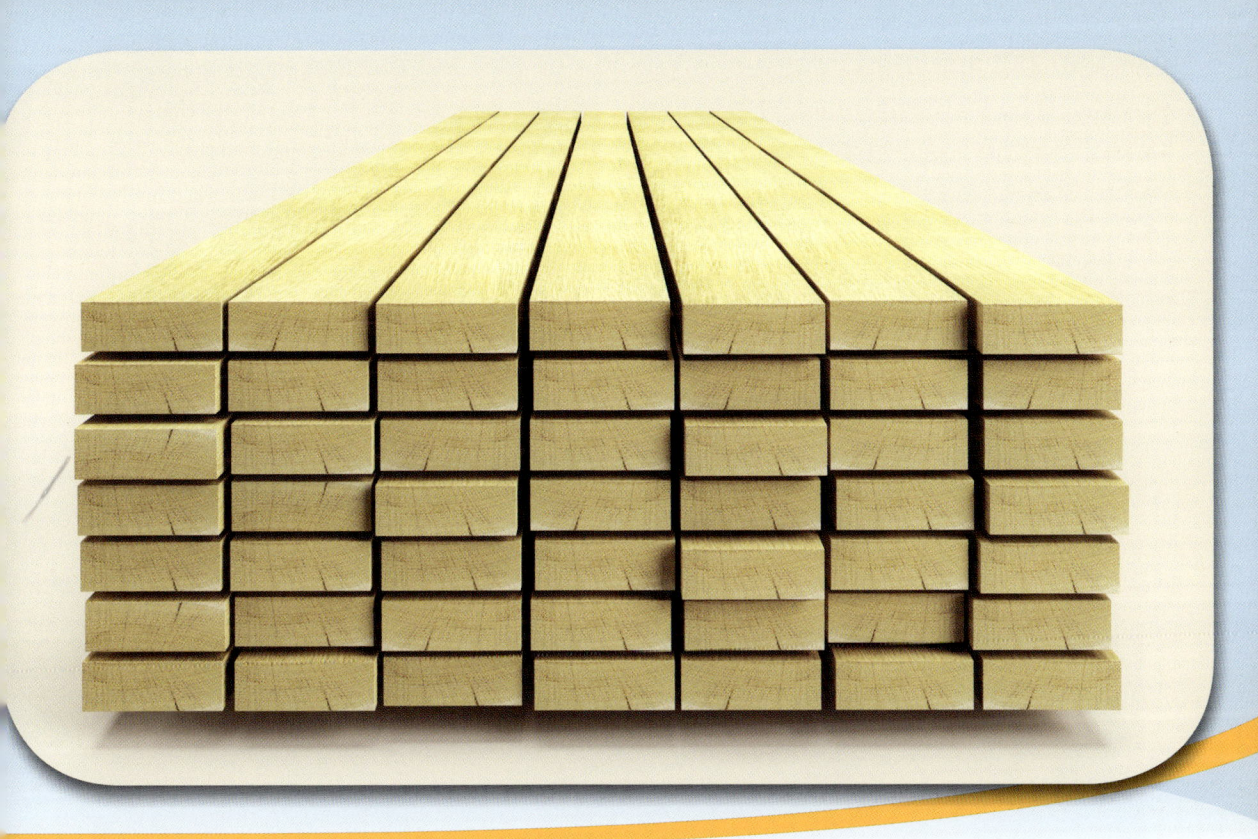

A fairground may need an extra shed, a new barn, or a concert stage from time to time. Lumber is a useful building material. Almost all pieces of lumber have the shape of a rectangular prism. We call these boards. Boards come in several common widths and heights, but their lengths often vary.

Sometimes, boards are stacked and tied into rectangular bundles. A bundle holds seven rows of seven boards. Each board measures 2 inches by 12 inches by 216 inches. What is the volume of one board? What is the volume of the stack of boards?

Visitors to a fairground can also see fruit, vegetable, and flower shows. People compete to grow the most perfect examples of their plants.

Different types of plants are judged in "divisions." One example of a division is Giant Vegetables. Within a division, each kind of vegetable or plant is called a "class." Classes of giant vegetables include giant cabbages, potatoes, squashes, tomatoes, and watermelon. However, giant pumpkins are probably the most famous kind of giant. One giant pumpkin can weigh more than 1,000 pounds!

A farmer wins a first-place ribbon for growing a huge pumpkin. The pumpkin is about 4 feet wide, 3 feet long, and 3 feet tall.

After the contest, the farmer looks for a wheelbarrow to carry the pumpkin back to her truck. The wheelbarrow can hold a load with a volume up to six cubic feet. Will the pumpkin fit in the wheelbarrow?

Deliveries

During the year, a variety of delivery trucks travel to and from fairgrounds. Trucks carry supplies for food stands and cleaning crews. Trucks carry sound and musical equipment for concerts. They carry game wheels and food booths. They carry lumber for building projects. Some trucks carry animals and feed for the animals, too.

A truck delivers hay to a barn. Another truck delivers some prize-winning goats. The truck with the hay is 40 feet long, 8 feet wide, and 12 feet tall. The truck with the goats is half as long, half as wide, and half as tall as the truck with the hay. How much more space is in the truck with hay than in the truck with goats?

Animal trailers include ramps for animals to enter and exit the trailers.

18

Many fairgrounds have space to hold thousands of visitors at a time. With so many people and so many events, fairgrounds are often noisy places. So, sets of loudspeakers can appear at locations around a fairground. Each speaker takes in electrical signals from microphones and recordings.

A loudspeaker changes the signals it gets from musical instruments and microphones into physical vibrations, or back-and-forth movements. Those vibrations move through the air and into our ears. Our brains interpret the vibrations so that we hear sounds.

In a crowded place like a fairground, one speaker may not be powerful enough to produce enough sound for a crowd to hear. But loudspeakers can be connected to get the job done. One loudspeaker is two feet long, three feet wide, and four feet tall. How much space do 10 loudspeakers, stacked in pairs, take up?

Winter Wonders

Winter fairgrounds attract people who have a variety of interests. Some visit for outdoor activities, like ice bowling, snow slides, and even mini-golf on a snow course. In many states, winter weather means very cold temperatures. Temperatures may stay below freezing, or less than 32° F (0° C). Cold temperatures outside can lead to a creative outdoor event called ice carving.

Ice carvers, or ice **sculptors**, carve objects and buildings. Ice sculptures may be as small as a dinner plate or as large as a hotel building. Most sculptures carved for events like those at a fairground stand from three to five feet tall. They may weigh more than 500 pounds.

Some ice is cloudy white. Other ice is clear. The color depends on how the ice is made. Ice sculptors prefer clear ice, which forms when water is allowed to move or circulate during the freezing process. Clear ice, however, is much more expensive to make. So, it costs sculptors more money.

A sculptor works with two blocks of ice to make a small sculpture. Each 11-pound block is 4.5 inches wide, 8.75 inches long, and 10 inches tall. How much space do both blocks take up before the sculptor begins carving?

Ice sculptors use tools, like chain saws, to help carve designs into the thick blocks of ice.

The time artists have to create ice statues or buildings is different from place to place. It all depends on how long the weather stays cold. Some locations have very cold weather for only a few days at a time. In other places, the outside temperatures may stay below freezing for months at a time.

With less time, ice carvers can only make smaller images. If they work in a place that has cold temperatures for weeks or months at a time, they can make bigger works of art. In a few places around the world, ice carvers even create working hotels. The rooms have walls, floors, and ceilings of ice. They even have ice beds. Guests staying in the hotel wrap themselves in heavy blankets before going to sleep.

While some visitors enjoy the outdoor winter events at the fairgrounds, others prefer to visit a variety of indoor exhibits, such as model railroad conventions.

Model railroads are often miniature worlds filled with far more than trains. There are tiny landscapes for the model trains to cross. There are bridges and tunnels. There are communities made of small buildings and even smaller people and animals.

Guests not only come to see the railroad displays, but they also visit the large number of vendors. **Vendors** sell various products, such as model railroad tools and parts.

This model railroad exhibit includes a busy train station.

Vendors rent space inside an exhibit hall. A vendor chooses a space that measures six feet by four feet. Then, he puts up portable walls, or walls that can be moved from place to place. The walls are each six feet tall and join at the corners. What is the volume of the vendor's exhibit space?

The vendor rents an additional space directly behind him. He uses the four feet by four feet floor space to store boxes of railroad parts. The walls are the same height as in the sales area. How much combined space did the vendor rent?

MATH AT WORK

Every year, people hire professional movers to move their family or business to a new location. Professional moving companies employ people to do several different jobs. All of the employees must understand volume.

If a family or business contacts a moving company, professional movers visit to look at what needs to be transported. These workers calculate the volume of furniture that will go into a truck. They also calculate the number and volume of cardboard boxes necessary to pack smaller items. This information determines what size truck the company needs to provide. A truck with the correct volume will hold everything that a family or business wants to move. But, it will not have so much volume that space goes unused.

Professional movers consider a number of things before deciding how much to charge a customer. First, they consider the size of the moving truck. Then, there is the weight of the load the truck will carry. Next, there is distance to consider. Movers calculate how far the truck will travel and how much gasoline will be required to complete the trip. There are other calculations, too, such as taxes. All of these costs are put into a single bill given to the customer.

Spring Blooms

Spring often brings changes to a fairground. Many plants begin to make flowers, and garden shows and contests become popular. Gardeners bring their best plants and flowers for everyone to see.

A gardening show at the fairgrounds can be large enough to take up space both inside and outdoors. To prepare for an outdoor garden show, fairground workers dig ditches to lay pipes for watering the plants. Workers dig a ditch 50 feet long. The ditch is three feet wide. If the workers remove 450 cubic feet of dirt, how many feet deep is the ditch?

 What's the Word?

Many gardeners grow flowers called pansies. The word *pansy* comes from the French word *pensée*, meaning "to think or remember." Some people describe the inner parts of a pansy's petals as faces. Those faces encourage some gardeners to be thoughtful or reflective.

Even the birds in this garden show are made of flowers.

Soap makers use a variety of plants to add scents to their soaps.

Not only are garden plants exhibited at the show, but some people also bring homemade goods to sell. For example, people use parts of flowers and plants to make and sell homemade soaps. Sometimes the garden show also holds a contest to find which vendor makes the best or most unique homemade goods.

Making soap from scratch is a long and exact process. It involves a recipe, ingredients, and cooking equipment. After melting, stirring, cooking, and cooling all of the ingredients, makers pour the soap into molds. As the soap cools, it turns to a solid. Once it is solid, it can be cut into bars.

A soap mold measures 20 inches by 15 inches by 2 inches. What is the mold's volume?

A soap maker cuts bars of soap from the mold. The bars are the same size. Each bar measures three inches by two inches by one inch. What is the volume of one bar of soap? How many bars of soap did the soap maker get from one mold?

Another spring event is hot-air balloon conventions. Fairgrounds often have large, open spaces that can be filled with hundreds of hot-air balloons. Riders step into baskets and travel up and down above the field.

A hot-air balloon has two main parts. The colorful part that fills with hot air is called the **envelope**. An envelope is made of the same kind of material as a parachute. The size of the envelope depends on the number of people the hot-air balloon is designed to carry.

The "basket" is the other main part of a hot-air balloon. The pilot and passengers ride in the basket. The size of the basket determines how many people it can carry.

At these events, colorful hot-air balloons can fill the sky above a fairground both day and night. At night, many pilots will **inflate**, or blow up, the envelopes to make them glow in the dark.

A hot-air balloon basket is a real basket. Many are made from woven, natural plant materials. Others are made of plastic or aluminum. Every basket material must be lightweight, strong, and able to survive rough landings.

Baskets come in a variety of sizes depending on how many people a pilot wants to carry at one time. Two to four passengers are common. But some baskets hold up to 20 passengers.

A basket manufacturer makes baskets in a variety of sizes. The most popular basket is 6 feet long, 4 feet wide, and 5 feet tall. So, the manufacturer keeps a supply on hand at all times. There are four stacks of baskets, with three baskets in each stack. How much space do the baskets take up in the manufacturer's storeroom?

Pet shows are also popular spring events at fairgrounds. There are often separate shows for dogs and cats. But, there are also shows for other pets, such as rabbits, guinea pigs, lizards, and turtles.

Pet shows may include contests for who has the best pet of its kind. Shows may also display supplies people need for keeping their pets healthy and happy. For example, some rabbit owners keep their pets in small structures called **hutches**.

A hutch is made of two stacked rectangular prisms. What is a method for finding the volume of both prisms?

Bearded dragons are native to Australia.

At a pet show, judges have to be able to see the animals easily. Animals such as rabbits and guinea pigs stay in cages. Other pets must be brought and kept in glass tanks. These pets may include lizards, snakes, and tarantulas.

Pet show organizers have to plan space for cages and tanks. So, they need to know the volumes of different cages and tanks. The bigger the animal, the bigger the volume of the container it will need during the show.

Most kinds of lizards do not need huge amounts of space to be safe and healthy. Bearded dragons are a friendly and calm kind of lizard. They are also relatively easy to care for, so they are popular pets.

A fairground's rules require that each adult bearded lizard live in a tank no smaller than 48 inches long, 13 inches wide, and 17 inches tall. Three contestants enter the bearded dragon contest. Two of the contestants have tanks that meet the minimum requirements. The third contestant's tank measures 52 inches by 14 inches by 20 inches. What is the combined volume of the bearded dragon tanks?

The Space Needle stands in Seattle, Washington.

CONNECTING TO HISTORY

From the 1870s through the 1930s, international fairs were held yearly in countries all over the world. Many of these international events have their own individual names, but are commonly called World's Fairs. A World's Fair may last as long as six months. It focuses on art, inventions, gardening, and agriculture.

People often build huge structures for a World's Fair. Many of those structures are temporary buildings. They remain standing only as long as the fair is open. However, some buildings are permanent and become symbols of the city in which they were built. For example, the Space Needle in Seattle was built for the 1962 World's Fair. It is a now a major tourist attraction. It has become a symbol of the city of Seattle. The Seattle Center Monorail was also built for the World's Fair and still operates daily.

A Ferris wheel is a common ride at fairgrounds.

In 1893, Chicago hosted a World's Fair called the Columbian Exposition. Grover Cleveland was the president of the United States at the time, and he opened the fair. Electricity was not yet in use in daily life. Companies competed for the right to provide lights and electricity at the fair, which ran for six months. During this time, more than 25 million people visited from all over the world.

There were lots of shows and sights at and next to the fair. One show was Buffalo Bill's Wild West Show, where Annie Oakley thrilled crowds with her shooting ability.

Chicago was the first World's Fair with an amusement area separate from the other buildings and exhibitions. The Ferris wheel and other attractions were located in the amusement area. The amusements were on either side of a mile-long strip called the Midway Plaisance. Today, this same kind of strip at any fair of any size is called the midway.

Here Comes Summer

State fairs are the biggest fairground event of the year. Most state fairs start in late summer and last from a week to a month. As summer begins, people who plan to enter contests are already working hard. They're training and caring for their animals. They're making sure their flowers, fruits, and vegetables are growing well. They're getting ready for the exciting summer events at the grounds.

Some state fairs have a parade. Riders may roll down the midway in antique cars. Or, they may march or ride horses.

Owners often buy or rent horse trailers to transport their horses to a fair. Twenty horse trailers are parked side by side along one wall of an exhibit hall. The trailers are identical, each measuring 10 feet long, six feet wide, and seven feet high. How much space do the trailers take up?

State fairs almost always have a canning contest. "Canning" is a processing method that turns many fruits and vegetables into jams and jellies. The name suggests the use of cans, but canning today is done in glass jars.

People invent original recipes, turning all kinds of fruits, vegetables, and plant parts into delicious spreads. By the end of summer, contest participants may have many jars of jam or jelly to enter into a contest.

A jelly maker buys one box of medium sized canning jars and a box of small canning jars. The larger box is 20 inches long, 16 inches wide, and 6 inches tall. Each dimension of the smaller box is half as great. What is the total volume of both boxes?

This display shows jars of honey, honeycomb, and a honey dipper. Many people use a wooden honey dipper to scoop honey from a jar.

Another popular food at state fairs is honey. Honey often has its own contest, and is judged differently than canned foods.

Honey contests may include foods baked or cooked with honey. People may show hives or beeswax. The contest may also include carvings made from beeswax, or other art related to bees and honey.

The key to harvesting good honey is timing. Months before the fair, bees are still making honey. Beekeepers have to wait through the summer to see how much honey is ready. They also have to leave enough for the bees to use the next winter.

Bee boxes can be moved and replaced, letting beekeepers manage the size of the hives inside.

Did You Know?

In the United States, there is an organization called the **Apiary** Inspectors of America. An apiary is a beehive. Apiary inspectors are hired by state governments to take care of bee farms in each state.

Modern beehives are shaped like boxes, so they're sometimes called "bee boxes." Stacks of bee boxes are set on blocks or wood to keep them off the ground.

Each bee box has parts, or sections, that can be removed. The sections where bees make honey are called "honey supers." Beekeepers remove the honey supers to harvest honey.

One bee box is 18 inches long, 16 inches wide, and 32 inches tall. Another has twice the volume. What is the volume of both boxes?

The Main Event

Finally, the end of summer arrives, but the weather is still warm and the days are sunny. In many states, it's time for the state fair!

Animal barns are some of the most popular places at a state fair. The barns are huge, holding hundreds of animals on any one day. The barns are divided into pens to keep groups of animals apart.

The size of a pen depends on the size of the animals that stay in it. A typical pen for adult goats, for example, is 8 feet long, 8 feet wide, and 4 feet tall.

A baby goat is called a kid.

During a young animal contest, baby goats played inside eight goat pens. The baby goats moved freely in their adult-sized pens. How much space do the goat pens take up in the barn?

At state fairs, there are many animal contests. Different kinds of animals are judged at a state fair, including cows, pigs, chickens, sheep, goats, and llamas. These animals are all called livestock. The word *livestock* describes animals that people use to earn money. Owners may sell their animals' milk, eggs, wool, or meat.

This sheep is a winner.

People don't normally sell or buy livestock at a state fair. Instead, they go to the fair to learn about livestock. Livestock contests are fun and educational. People learn how to care for animals and how to show them at fairs.

What do the judges look for? They look at an animal's muscles to see that the animal is healthy and well grown. They want to see how well formed the animal's skeleton is. They can tell this by the animal's size and how it stands. Judges also look for how smoothly an animal moves and how neat and clean it looks.

Food stands are also popular at state fairs. Many visitors enjoy fair foods, such as sandwiches, lemonade, candy, and desserts.

One favorite fairground snack is popcorn. Most popcorn supplied around the world is grown in the United States. And although worldwide popularity of popcorn is growing, U.S. citizens eat more popcorn per person than any other group of people.

In one year, sales of uncooked popcorn reached almost one billion dollars in the U.S. Most popcorn buyers cook their popcorn at home. But that still leaves plenty of popcorn to cook and sell at fairgrounds and other entertainment centers.

A popcorn vendor buys bags of uncooked popcorn. The bags arrive in shipping boxes 2 feet long, 2 feet wide, and 2 feet high. Boxes fill 64 cubic feet of space inside her food booth. How many boxes of popcorn does the vendor have?

Funnel cakes attract many hungry visitors at a state fair. Makers let cake batter drip through a funnel into hot oil. The oil sizzles as the batter cooks into a crispy brown finish. The maker scoops up the cake, slides it onto a plate, and sprinkles it with powdered sugar.

Cotton candy is another popular fair treat. Some cotton candy makers make the spools of sugar in a machine while you wait. Others buy it from candy companies and sell it in plastic bags.

A candy company has three shipping sizes of cotton candy. A small box is three feet by two feet by two feet. Each dimension of the medium box is twice as long. And each dimension of the large box is three times as great. What's the volume of the largest shipping box?

Carnival rides may not have always been part of every state fair. However, they are definitely very popular now! There may be merry-go-rounds for younger children and giant slides and bumper cars for people of all ages. Some rides are only for older visitors. These are usually the ones that go extremely fast or turn riders upside down.

People buy tickets to ride carnival rides. Tickets are small colorful pieces of stiff paper. Rides may require more than one ticket to ride. People can use their tickets to play carnival games, too. Games give players chances to win stuffed animals and other prizes.

Rolls of tickets are delivered to a ticket booth in two separate cardboard boxes. Each box is four feet long, three feet wide, and two feet high. How much space do both boxes take up?

After months of preparation and many days of exciting contests, rides, and activities, a state fair eventually comes to an end. Contestants collect their ribbons and prizes. Livestock and pet owners load their animals into trucks or cars to take them home.

Employees of the fairground help visitors make their way to the exits. They help clean up the fields, barns, and buildings. Finally, the fair is closed and the last people leave.

Then, it's time for the fall events once again and another season of fun at the fairgrounds!

iMath IDEAS: What's the Volume?

At the end of the state fair, a carousel owner decides to move his carousel to a new fairground. He will take the carousel apart and rent a truck to carry it to its new home.

The carousel's wooden animals are wrapped in moving blankets. The roof comes down and its pieces are unfastened for shipping. Poles are bundled for easy moving.

The owner calls a rental company to find out about truck sizes. If he can, he wants to put everything on one truck. If that's not possible, he will rent more than one truck.

The owner estimates that ten carousel horses take up 320 cubic feet of space in all. The inside of the largest truck he can rent is 25 feet long, eight feet wide, and eight feet tall. How much space will be left over after all of the horses are put on the truck? How can he find out?

Idea 1: He can **model** volume. But it's unlikely the owner has cubes to measure or the time to solve the problem this way.

43

Idea 2: He can use a **formula**. The owner can use the formula $V = \ell \times w \times h$ to find the truck's volume.

$$25 \text{ feet} \times 8 \text{ feet} \times 8 \text{ feet} = ? \text{ cubic feet (ft}^3\text{)}$$

But this measurement alone won't give him the information he needs.

Idea 3: Once the owner knows the truck's volume, he can **use an operation** to find out how much space will be left in the truck after he loads 10 carousel horses. The horses, remember, have a volume of 320 cubic feet (ft³).

The owner wants to know how much space will be left over, which means he will need to subtract to find the answer.

The truck's total volume − 320 cubic feet (ft³) = ?

How much space will be left over?

This carousel will join new rides and games at a different fairground. But its new home will be much like its old one. There will be visitors throughout the year, enjoying the events, rides, food, and lights of another busy fairground.

WHAT COMES NEXT?

Ask your friends and family members to think about what they would like to see or do if they visited a fairground. What kinds of rides would they want to ride? Which kinds of games would they want to play? Use their ideas to design a new ride or game that you think they might enjoy.

If you design a ride, what kind of ride would it be? What would it look like? How many people could ride at one time? What would the rules be?

Draw a sketch of your ride or game. Determine its length, width, and height. How much space will the ride or game require?

Give your ride or game an exciting name. Share your idea with friends and family members. Working together, you might make a model of your ride or game.

GLOSSARY

apiary: a beehive.

cubic unit: a unit used to measure volume or capacity. The sides of a cube are all squares.

dimension: a measure in a direction, such as length, width, or height.

dressage: a set of movements made by a horse at a rider's command.

envelope: the colorful part of a hot-air balloon that fills with heated air.

estimate: to make a guess based on available information.

face: one side of a solid figure. A cube, for example, has six square faces.

formula: a mathematical rule written with symbols.

hutch(es): a pen or housing structure for animals, like rabbits.

inflate: to fill with air or another gas.

livestock: animals that are raised and sold for money.

maze: a network of paths that people find their way through.

model: something that stands for something else. It can also mean to use objects to make calculations.

operation: a mathematical action which produces a new value, such as addition, subtraction, multiplication, or division.

rectangular prism: a prism with six faces that are all rectangles.

sculptor(s): someone who carves wood, clay, ice, or other material.

vendor(s): someone who sells goods or services.

volume: how much space an object takes up, or how many cubic units fill it.

FURTHER READING

FICTION
Project Mulberry, by Linda Sue Park, Clarion Books, 2005
True Blue, by Jane Smiley, Knopf Books for Young Readers, 2011

NONFICTION
Figuring Out Geometry, by Rebecca Wingard-Nelson, Enslow Publishers, 2008
The Hive Detectives: Chronicle of a Honey Bee Catastrophe, by Loree Griffin Burns, Houghton Mifflin, 2010

ADDITIONAL NOTES

The page references below provide answers to questions asked throughout the book. Questions whose answers will vary are not addressed.

Page 13: The volume of one bale is 15,552 cubic inches (in^3). The volume of four identical bales is 62,208 cubic inches (in^3).

Page 14: The shed has a volume of 1,200 cubic feet (ft^3). $1,200 - 800 = 400$ cubic feet (ft^3)

Page 15: One board has a volume of 2 inches $\times$ 12 inches $\times$ 216 inches = 5,184 cubic inches (in^3). 5,184 cubic inches (in^3) $\times$ 49 boards = 254,016 cubic inches (in^3).

Page 17: The pumpkin has a volume of about 36 cubic feet (ft^3). No, the pumpkin will not fit in the wheelbarrow.

Page 18: The volume of the feed truck is 3,840 cubic feet (ft^3). The volume of the truck carrying the goats is 480 cubic feet (ft^3). The larger truck has 3,360 cubic feet (ft^3) more space.

Page 19: The volume of one speaker is 2 feet $\times$ 3 feet $\times$ 4 feet = 24 cubic feet (ft^3). 24 cubic feet $\times$ 10 speakers = 240 cubic feet (ft^3)

Page 20: One block has a volume of 393.75 cubic inches (in^3). Two identical blocks have a combined volume of 787.5 cubic inches (in^3).

Page 22: The original space has a volume of 144 cubic feet (ft^3). The additional space has a volume of 96 cubic feet (ft^3). Together, they take up 240 cubic feet (ft^3) of space.

Page 24: $50 \times 3 \times x = 450$ cubic feet (ft^3). $x = 3$ feet.

Page 25: The mold's volume is 600 cubic inches (in^3). A bar's volume is 6 cubic inches (in^3). The mold produced 100 bars of soap.

Page 27: 1,440 cubic feet (ft^3)

Page 28: One method for finding volume: Measure the length, width, and height of one of the prisms. Calculate its volume. Then, multiply the volume by two to determine the volume of the entire hutch.

Page 29: 35,776 cubic inches (in^3)

Page 32: 8,400 cubic feet (ft^3)

Page 33: 1,920 cubic inches (in^3) + 240 cubic inches (in^3) = 2,160 cubic inches (in^3)

Page 35: 9,216 cubic inches (in^3) + 18,432 cubic inches (in^3) = 27,648 cubic inches (in^3)

Page 36: 2,048 cubic feet (ft^3)

Page 38: 8 boxes

Page 39: 324 cubic feet (ft^3)

Page 40: 48 cubic feet (ft^3)

Page 44: 1,600 cubic feet (ft^3); 1,600 cubic feet (ft^3) − 320 cubic feet (ft^3) = 1,280 cubic feet (ft^3)

INDEX

apiary, 35
bearded dragon, 29
beekeepers, 34–35
canning, 33
carousel, 42–44
Chicago World's Fair of 1893, 31
cubic units, 6, 11
dimension, 7, 33, 39
dressage, 12
envelope, 26
estimate, 10, 43
face, 8, 24
Ferris wheel, 5, 31
formula, 8–9, 11, 44
funnel cakes, 39
honey, 5, 34–35
hot-air balloons, 26–27
hutch(es), 28
ice carving, 20
inflate, 26
livestock, 5, 37, 41

maze, 14
Midway Plaisance, 31
model, 7, 43, 45
model railroad, 22
operation, 9, 11, 44
pet shows, 28–29
professional movers, 23
rectangular prisms, 8, 10, 15, 28
sculptor(s), 20–21
Seattle (Washington, USA), 30
Seattle Center Monorail, 30
Space Needle, 30
vendor(s), 22, 25, 38
volume, 6–9, 11, 13, 15, 17, 22–23, 25, 28–29, 33, 35, 39, 42–44

CONTENT CONSULTANT

David T. Hughes

David is an experienced mathematics teacher, writer, presenter, and adviser. He serves as a consultant for the Partnership for Assessment of Readiness for College and Careers. David has also worked as the Senior Program Coordinator for the Charles A. Dana Center at The University of Texas at Austin and was an editor and contributor for the *Mathematics Standards in the Classroom* series.